Searching Within

Austyn Fisher

I0141012

Dedicated to those who are
struggling

Cover is designed using canva.com.

10 9 8 7 6 5 4 3 2 1

ISBN: 979-8-9857414-9-0

Sections

Mental

Flower

The petals fall

As I droop down

Wilting away

Collapsing down, slowly

I'm losing my color

Becoming brown

No longer beautiful

I'm dying

I have lost everything

My spirit

The glorious smell

Goodbye divine

It's dark all around

Footsteps on me

I'm forgotten

Under a white sheet

Suddenly the light is peaking

Moisture all around

The sheet is melting

A bud appears

My leaves are green

My cherished colors

So vibrant

I'm alive

I've survived

The darkness

And people see

The petals grow

Feel

Allow yourself to feel everything.

Change or control

I don't know anymore

Pink, purple, or blue

Not a single clue

The relief

Only lasts a week

Is it too taboo

Mess all around

A hair color yet to be found

Talking all around but I can't hear

Breathing heavily without a pause

Am I going to die

Oh no here comes a tear

I'm not thinking clear

The intense pressure on my chest

I can't move, frozen in time

Is the end near

There's ringing in my ear

Please please make it stop

I'm spinning

There's so much fear

With talking all around but I can't hear

Take a deep breath

In and out

Slow and steady

Everything will be alright

Hug

No one knows how much a hug

Can truly relieve your pain.

Why do I feel pretty?

But tear myself down

Why do I feel ugly?

But complement my eyes

Why am I this way?

When no one can relate

Why am I weird?

When I desire to be normal

Why must I be like this?

Makeup

I hide under this layer

Not an imperfection to be seen

This is better, this makes me pretty

Yet it feels like it puts me in a shell

That I can wipe off.

Sleep

All my problems disappear

When the eyes close

My mind is clear

Yet I still awake with fear

I'm not good enough

That is all I hear

I've been slipping the past year

But when my head hits the pillow

All my problems disappear

Survive

Surviving is not living

And living is not surviving

If you understand the difference

I'm sorry, keep fighting.

I'm in your corner

Empty

Ice cold, numb

A shell of a body

Not able to feel

Containing nothing

But a racing mind

And a slow heartbeat

In a dark room

Silent, not a sound

Except for my thoughts

Are so loud, it hurts

They never stop

Pounding in my head

Heartbeats faster

And I let it out

I scream and tears fall

But no one hears

I never want to see the light of day

This is what the thoughts tell me

Maybe they are right

I should end it all

Make it all stop

For I'm in a dark room

Surrounded by my thoughts

With no one to hear because

I am alone in silence

Not a sound to hear

The cry for help

With a blade so cold

The first sigh of relief

Yet I'm so numb

Don't do it I was told

But no one cares

While I'm in my room alone

Not feeling bold

I don't matter

Does anyone matter

Or is the world in a blindfold

No one will miss me

All I need is a hug

How will this all unfold

I just want this end

But will anyone listen

I'm sorry, I couldn't go on

It's not your fault

This world was too cruel

I was lost

I couldn't find myself

I needed to leave

This was the only answer

The pain wouldn't stop

There's was no way out

The world never cared

It was crashing down

 And I was drowning

Drowning in my thoughts

The blood that dripped

Wasn't enough

I needed more

It was never enough

I wasn't enough

Don't blame yourself

You were the one that cared

You wrapped me in my arms

I was safe

But once you let go

The shadows arrived

The demons

Lit a fire in my soul

The voices wouldn't stop

I cried for help

But it wasn't enough

No one listened

Just think of me

As the dandelion

That blew away

Flatline

The alarm sounds

There's crying all around

It's over

The burden's dead

But now there's dread

Eating

Mirror, Mirror

I sit there staring
With a reflection looking back.
Just look at me comparing

How is this society?
Can't we all just be happy
It's too much for my anxiety

Do looks really matter
Of course, they do
People don't care if you shatter

They just want to feel good
Can't we stop this cycle
 Everyone's just misunderstood

Mirror, mirror
Please tell me why!

Sexy

I'm supposed to be sexy

With a thin waist with curves for days

An hour glass per say

Anything but, isn't good enough

What is sexy because

I'm not it.

I'm convinced

I'm not perfect

I'm not skinny

I'm not sexy

I'm not beautiful

I'm convinced

I am flawed

I am too fat

I am repulsive

I am ugly

Bikini

Not enough

No boobs, no butt

Skinny but it doesn't fit

Too much

Big boobs, big butt

Curvy but it doesn't fit

Grabbing one here

Grabbing one there

Snack after snack

Weight goes up

Pound by pound

Looking down

Tears fall

One by one

Yet I can't stop

I'm afraid

My body is developing

It's forming curves

I'm gaining weight

I'm curvy but all I see is fat

So I change it

If I see fat I get rid of it

I'm getting thinner and thinner

But it's not enough

I must do more

Now I see a skeleton

I don't like this look either

I'm nothing but bones

I can't live like this

So I know what to do

My curves are coming back

I don't know how I feel

But I've learned a few things along the way

Curvy or skinny, I'm beautiful

As long as I'm healthy

I will try anything

To be skinnier

But I keep getting bigger

I can't stop eating

Its a war inside myself

I will try anything

To be curvier

But I keep getting smaller

I can't stop starving

Size

Have you ever got so overwhelmed

With clothes shopping

Trying not to cry in the dressing room

While you force yourself into the smaller size

Trying to hide your panic when handed a

size two

Scale

One foot, then the other

I watch the numbers rise

As my self-esteem falls

The climbing stops

As I see my size

I go numb

From the number

on the scale

Hiding

Food Disappears

But it wasn't eaten

Some in the trash

Some under covers

Can't be seen

Out of sight

Out of mind

I won't eat

I can't eat

Just keep hiding

Diet Pills

It gives me a grip

They claim they cleanse

I don't care if they work

For all I see is away

Out of my thoughts

Secret

My family never knew

I kept it a secret

I would throw away food

Became too obsessed with calories

And watching them burn

Telling them I'm not hungry

And locking myself away

Went to the gym because of guilt

The lower the number the better

Became stronger and weaker

I was doing it for all the wrong reasons

Not to feel good but to feel lighter

Freaking out when the numbers rose

But my family new knew

Calories

100, 200, and more

Tracking, counting

I've been down this road before

Running

Subtracting one by one

200, 100, down, and down

Having an uncontrollable craving

But I must eat, not

Food in front of me

I'm constantly starving

Starving

I can't eat

It hurts

Only a taste

Will do

I don't feel hunger

Yet I'm starving

I can taste

But I can't eat

Bones

Running my fingers

Along my bones

Ridges and valleys

Light as a feather

But feeling like stones

Sweatshirt

Cloaked in cloth

Hiding all imperfections

No one can see

Everything that is me

Cloaked in cloth

Baggy with a hood on top

No one can see

Because a sweatshirt

Is hiding me

Model

She's so pretty

She's put together

She's successful

She's perfect

But after that camera shot

She's crying herself to sleep

She's falling apart

She's fighting for her job

She's just like you and me

Liar

Sometimes the mirror shows you beauty,

But you see a lie.

Love

Saving the Strays

I am a savior.

Giving a gateway

From their disorderly behavior

But I'm just a throwaway

Confidence.

It's all they need to leave

Just a little reassurance

Now I gotta grieve

I become their ashtray

They leave me in the dust

They leave me as the prey

I thought it was all trust

Now I'm scared to be attached

Every man for himself

Unless you're unmatched

Why me why not anybody else?

So come one, come all

The door's open

I'm saving the strays.

Hold Me

You make me feel safe in your arms

Wrapping me up so tight as we fall asleep

Please, hold me forever and forever

I never want this to end

As I feel safe in your arms.

I watch you

As you drove away

A kiss goodbye

And a bear hug

Not letting go

Hearing you heart

Warms mine

 And I feel safe

Said I love you

As you turned away

And turned the key

With a simple wave

I closed your door

And walked away

I won't see you

For awhile

Please be safe

I need you here

With me

Forever and always

Snow Globe

Under the mistletoe

Standing, waiting

Seeing your shadow

My cheeks begin to thaw

With a nose so cold

You leave me in awe

My stomach-turning

Like a shaken globe

With love burning

Climb

I climbed a mountain,

 to get to you.

Once I reached the top

You grabbed my hand.

And we looked a little farther

Ups and downs, twists and turns

We are climbing this mountain called

Love.

That Girl

I've never been that girl

Surprises and roses

Grab my hand and twirl

Hopeless romantic

Feeling like a princess

In panic

Can't be contained

With a heart so full

But now I've explained

I am that girl

Necklace

You grabbed the chain

As I pulled my hair way

Clipping it to my neck

You gave me your first

Until I can have your last.

Sex

I was scared

for you to touch my skin

Giving me goosebumps

And sending shivers

A gentle fingertip

Caressing my back

As I lay on your chest

A look and a soft kiss

Leading to intensity

But then you leave

And for the next guy

Is it just a matter of time?

Love

While I don't show it well

Just remember I love you.

Dark hair

With a bitty waist

So talented

So much better

Beautiful stunning

Something I can't match

I'm nothing

Compared to the girl

With the dark hair

Shattered

You picked the piece off the ground

You glued them back together

The pieces became whole

Then you took it with your words and

crushed it

You were the reason the pieces broke

Again and again.

Your Words

Picking me up

Making my stomach flutter

Hearing beautiful come off your lips

You were my reason to smile.

Tearing me down

Making my stomach turn

Hearing ugly come off your lips

You were my reason to cry.

Manipulation

You had an abusive dad

You wanted to kill yourself

You were misunderstood by the world

You wanted someone to listen

But it changed to

You want my body

You want to feel my warmth

You want to feel our lips touch

I really liked you

But I was scared

And forbidden

I wish I had listened

If you didn't get what you wanted

You told me you were done

 Not with me

But this thing called life

I gave you what you wanted

It kept you happy

I hated seeing you struggle

I knew you had a good heart

I dug and dug for it

I thought I had found it

But was it ever really there

I was blindsided

I saved you from a cold night

You cried to me

But I will never know

If those were real tears

We talked every day and night

I helped you be good in school

Things were looking up for you

I thought I made you happy

What was wrong with me

Holding your hand through it all

Letting our lips touch

But that wasn't enough

You wanted more and more

Everyone knew

But I told them they were wrong

That I knew the real you

I did stuff for you

That I would never do

I held your hand through it all

But I guess you didn't appreciate it

I held on while you slipped away

Did you ever actually care

I gave you everything

I tried to save you

And when you left

I was lost without you

I didn't understand, what did I do

I was there when no one else was

But you took advantage of me

I had a good heart

I let you in, I cared

But the only thing you did in return

Was manipulate me

You got what you wanted

Then you chewed me up and spit me out

I came crawling back

That's exactly what you wanted

I was wrapped around your finger

Begging at your feet

Are you happy now?

Losing You

Heart so broke

Face burning

Tears rolling down

I'm a mess

What did I do

To lose you

Self

Myself

All I have is myself

In this game one calls

Life

Picking myself back up

But I will fall again

No one will help

Dusting myself off

I get up and start again

Because in this game of life

All I have is myself

You

You are a mystery

A storm and a dream

You can be anything

Make and keep yourself happy

It's in your hands.

Deep

Look deep into your reflection

And see the suffering

Then wrap yourself in a hug

And let it go like the wind

Better

I know it doesn't seem like it

But you can get out of this hole

And you will be better than ever before

Tell your story

It's okay to talk about it

Reach out

Make a voice for yourself

You are better than your story

You can overcome it

With time and that's okay

Different

I may be different

But different is good

Embrace the differences

Your flaws

Are a part of you

Everyone has them

They make you

Simply you

Here a fat roll

A form of birth control

But he's a troll

I'm beautifully me

Finally free

He sees me with envy

Stretch Marks

Beautiful stripes

Like a majestic Zebra

Flowing down my body

Green

The grass is always greener

This I have found

I still slip to the winter

It's not always happiness all around

Growth is always better

But its okay to slip

But remember

The other side

Where the grass is always greener

Learning

There's a process

I may not know the steps

But I'm gaining knowledge

I research

How to be happy?

I wish it was that easy

It's a roller coaster

Emotionally and physically

I want to love myself

How do I change?

I take care of myself

But sometimes I fall

Everyone helps me

But I can only truly help myself

When will I be okay?

I woke up with a sense of relief

A smile on my face

A clear mind

And a body I'm taking care of

Am I better forever?

Smile

I used to think I wasn't good enough

I didn't belong in this world

I didn't attribute anything

It would be better if I was gone

I tried to end it all

Make it all disappear

Make me disappear

I don't deserve to live

I was a burden

I dragged people down with me

I hurt myself

I made other people suffer

I was ready to end it all

But I was taken by the hand

I was shown the way

By people I love

They cared enough to stay

To help me through it all

They helped me find myself

This is my reason to smile

Growth

I went from crying everyday

Then to every other day

Then to hardly any day

I went from tearing myself down

Then to hiding it better

Then to blocking it out

I went from hardly speaking

To finding one friend

Then finding more

I stopped activities

To starting with one

Then I was doing them all

I went from never being happy

To smiling every day

Then laughing

I may not have started well

But I built myself up

Little by little

Enough is tough

But remember

You are always

Tough and enough

Embrace

Embrace who you are

Embrace your flaws

Embrace your perfections

Embrace your attitude

Embrace your personality

Embrace your body

Embrace your hair

Embrace your emotion

Embrace you

Alive

Feeling my heartbeat

Tension washing away

A true smile

I'm okay

I've survived the storm

I'm finally alive

Perfect

Perfect doesn't exist,

You define it.

www.ingramcontent.com/pod-product-compliance
Lightning Source LLC
LaVergne TN
LVHW041234080426
835508LV00011B/1205